Testimonials for "A Life of Miracles"

Ani Amoore has been instrumental in praying for me throughout my life, including her prayers of bringing the right person into my life. Thank you Ani!!!!
— Nina Kouyoumdjian

A Life of Miracles *is a testimony to the power of love between two sisters in Christ, Sonia Kouyoumdjian and Ani Amoore. Thirty-six years ago, Christ the Lord generously gave us the gift of a "faith filled" friendship and a relationship that has been abundantly blessed, through the abundance of God's Grace! This is also a statement of praise for the answered prayer of Ani and Sonia for the life of Nina Kouyoumdjian, who miraculously was born, and resembles her beautiful Spiritual Godmother, Ani Amoore, in many ways. I also acknowledge Ani and her husband John, for their generosity in sharing God's love to the world around them, and for exemplifying the true meaning of Christian friendship, and faithfulness. I must acknowledge God as The One who brought the Kouyoumdjian and the Amoore family together into His flock through His Providential plan, shepherding us all through His Word and Spirit.* – Sonia Kouyoumdjian, February 6, 2017

A LIFE OF
MIRACLES

Genocide, Trials, Blessings,
and Loss—But Miracles All the Way

by *Ani Amoore*

with Don Huntington

A Life of Miracles
Copyright ©2017 Ani Amoore

First Edition April 2017

Park Place Publications
Pacific Grove, California
Printed in U S A

Photos from family archives

ISBN 978-1-943887-47-7

Cover image: Shutterstock "Magic Lotus Flower"
by Vadim Georgiev

Dedication

*I dedicate this book to the memory of my beloved
husband, John Amoore, who was a gift given to me
by the hand of a loving God. He was my best friend and
devoted husband for 35 years and the only love
of my life from the moment of our first kiss
until now, and forever.*

WITH SPECIAL THANKS TO MY CHILDREN

I especially want to acknowledge my daughter, Marie, above, and my son, Ronald, below, for always being there for me through my trials with aging.

Acknowledgments

The book came into being through the prompting and power of the Spirit of God. He laid the project on my heart for decades until finally giving me the green light to write down the memories and accounts of the things that happened to the people I love and to me that changed my life and the lives of many others.

God brought Laura Tabsharani into my life. She introduced me to the process by which a book is actually written and got me started. I thank my daughter, Marie, for encouraging me to write the book and especially for sharing with me a true vision that she had one night of my parents and others speaking to her from the Other Side telling her to make sure that I completed the project.

I especially thank Dr. Don Huntington who used a gift given him by God to help me find the right words to precisely record on paper the memories that had been burning in my heart for so many years.

Ani Amoore

Ani's children and grandchildren. Back row, left to right: Marie, Isabella, Ruth, Ron, Harout, and Alec. Front row, left to right: Kate, Johnny, Joey Amoore.

A Life of Miracles

The stories that you are about to read of the way that God moved in and through my life were uplifting, often miraculous, and always wonderful.

I tell you also that what you read about my life is absolutely true.

Ani's children: Ronald Amoore and Marie Amoore.

Contents

Dedication   *iii*

Acknowledgments   *v*

Summary of My Life   1

Introduction   3

CH. 1   MASSACRE AND SURVIVAL   *11*

CH. 2   MY CYPRIOT CHILDHOOD   *21*

CH. 3   A LOVE STORY   *37*

CH. 4   SERVING GOD, FAMILY, AND THE WORLD   *67*

CH. 5   ANSWERED PRAYER AND OTHER MIRACLES   *87*

Conclusion   STILL AWASH IN GRACE   *121*

Ani Amoore

A Life of Miracles

Summary of My Life

Jesus led me all the way,
Led me step by step each day;
I will tell the saints and angels as I lay my
  burdens down,
"Jesus led me all the way."
— John W. Peterson

INTRODUCTION

I've witnessed the power of prayer throughout a lifetime of sunny mountaintops of blessing and joy as well as dark valleys of loss and days of terrible suffering. During times of tears, hurt, and failure, I would ask God to show me a reason for the things that I was suffering. He didn't always show me His reason but always gave me His comfort. To the person of true faith, it is enough to simply know there is a reason, whether or not we know what the reason is.

The storms of life were always followed by times when the sunshine of God shown brilliantly, and I realized that the difficulties had strengthened me and made me more confident of His love and presence. After all, the stars only shine brightly in the darkest night and rainbows appear only following rainstorms.

The book has been 40 years in preparation. For decades, people have been blessed by the stories I would tell of the love of God and the miracles He performed in my life and on behalf of my family and the people whose lives I was able to touch. In many cases, my listeners were encouraged and spiritually refreshed by the things I would tell them. They would often say, "We will never forget what you told us, Ani!"

Many of them have been telling me that I ought to write a book in order to preserve the memories of the amazing things that I have witnessed and the wonderful insights about the ways of God and man that have come to me.

The production of this book is itself a good example of the way the Spirit of God has moved in my life. I've never made an important decision without taking the matter to the Lord. I remained in a state of prayer and waited upon Him until He gave me signs that made clear to me that the time had arrived to put down an account of how God is real and how He has directed every step, opening and closing doors that led me to the ways I could best serve Him through the decades of my life.

I wanted to get the memories recorded before they were gone forever, but never felt the time was right until I woke up one morning with the voice of God speaking to my heart a message, "It is time to write your book." It was so clear that I thought I might be losing my mind. However, I couldn't deny the fact that the voice of God, in fact, had come to me telling me that I needed to get started on the project. Like Gideon with the fleece, I put out tests for confirmation. The second came to pass the very same day when God put me in contact with a friend, Laura Tabsharani, who is working in the publishing industry. Laura showed me how to put the project together and connected me with a ghostwriter, Dr. Don Huntington, who turned out to be the perfect person to help me tell the story.

The third sign came the following morning when I turned on the TV and heard Rev. Joel Osteen declare that God can use a person at any stage of life. He then began to enumerate, saying that God could use people while they were in their 20s, 30s, 40s, 50s.... Then he skipped a decade and said that God could use us in our 70s. That was my category!

After we got started, the book was put on hold for a few months because of a serious illness on my part and scheduling conflicts. It might have remained on the back burner indefinitely, except that my daughter, Marie, had a dream one night. "Mom," she said. "I think you need to start the book again. Your parents and family members on the Other Side gave me a message to pass on to you.

They said, 'Tell your mother that she should finish the book and give copies to the grandchildren and to her loved ones.'"

In no way am I writing this book because I imagine myself to be an extraordinary person or some kind of saint. It hasn't always been easy to get out of the way and let the Spirit of God work freely through me. For one thing, I'm sensitive to the comments and attitudes of others. Sometimes I'm frightened and uncertain, thinking that other people might be right and I am wrong. I am afraid of hurting them and fearful that they will take things the wrong way. I've had problems with communications—imagining sometimes that people understand me but later discovering they didn't understand at all.

People have occasionally said hurtful things to me and at the beginning I would retreat from them socially. Rather than responding to criticism, I would just clam up. People would think I was stupid, so I learned that it is good sometimes to gently push back. People have also abused me, which made me cautious about getting too close too quickly. I tend to keep some distance; a conversation with three people sometimes feels safer and more comfortable than with two.

I also developed an early fear of death that lasted far into adulthood. My childhood friend, Shaké, shared my fears. We always felt we were sick and infirm. Starting at age 13, she and I would say every year, "We are going to die soon" and would actually cry bitter tears over our impending death. When I turned 20, I felt old and imagined that death was rapidly approaching. After Mom developed cancer, I was sure that I had cancer myself and for years maintained my lingering conviction that I would soon be dead and in my grave. Even after marriage, I announced to my husband that I would be dead soon. My attitude wasn't morose because I always thought I should have a good time since I probably wouldn't live very long. Now I'm in my 70s and still alive. John suffered through my hypochondria and, in fact, died long before me of cancer—the disease I had spent my lifetime fearing most.

However, for all my misgivings and self-doubts, I love to bring out the best in other people. I always search for something to genuinely compliment in others. It makes me happy to make someone else happy and especially to work with people who are infirm and needy—orphans and widows, whom the Bible declared to be worthy of special attention. However, success in being a positive force for encouragement and change requires discernment; being able to identify people who will understand and respond from those who will not or cannot.

Ani Amoore

There is nothing particularly extraordinary about my intelligence and gifts. Far from being saintly, I admit that I am a sinner and would be lost in the night had I had not spent decades in the service of a divine Master—one who has performed some astonishing miracles on my behalf and on behalf of those who God had introduced to me over the decades of my life. It would be a shame if those events should be swallowed up by time and the memory of those miracles be lost to the world.

In summary, my purpose in writing the story of my life is to leave for my children, grandchildren, and perhaps others an account of how God worked through me and perhaps come to believe that He can work through them, as well. This book is a testament of the faithfulness of God, who has been with me through the dark valleys of life as well as on the sunny mountaintops.

My mind is overflowing with memories of the events that have occurred throughout my seven decades. Some of them were wonderful almost beyond my ability to put into words. Other things happened, however, to me and to the people I love that were indescribable. However, the Lord always helped lead us through.

However, more than simply leaving behind a narrative of the history of my life, my larger purpose in creating this account is to convey a profound reality that has been with me from the beginning. Through all the events of my life—from the most wonderful success to the most terrible tragedy—a light from the face of God, shining through his Son has illuminated each of those circumstances ultimately shaping it for His glory and purpose. The light of God provides a brilliance that blots out any darkness or despair that the evil things otherwise would certainly have implanted in my Spirit. The light extinguishes any sense of pride or self-satisfaction that those miraculous occurrences might have created, as well

Jesus is real! He has been my constant companion and has answered prayers throughout the course of my life, guided me each step of the way. I pray that the words I have written will channel His light forward to people who might be reading these words long after I have passed from the scene.

CHAPTER 1

MASSACRE AND SURVIVAL

The 20th century witnessed a number of horrible mass killings, beginning in the second decade with the organized slaughter of Armenians by an Islamic despot named Sultan Abdul Hamid II, the last of the old Ottoman leaders. He instituted the extermination of the country's Armenian minority from their historic homeland through waves of summary executions. The Armenians were one of the world's most ancient Christian churches. A smaller number of members of other ethnic Christian groups such as the Assyrians and the Greeks were also caught up in the killings.

The wholesale slaughter was the first modern instance of mass killings on such a monstrous scale. The remnant who survived, came to refer to the killings by the simple term "the massacre," but the rest of the world came to refer to it by the term, "genocide," which was first coined precisely to describe what the Turks did to the Armenians.

The slaughter began In April 1915 with the arrest of some 250 Armenian intellectuals and community leaders in Constantinople. It ended when Mustafa Kemal, the founder of the Turkish nation, eradicated the Armenian population of the city of Anatolia. During the intervening eight years, the horror proceeded in two phases: The first involved the executions of the Armenian males followed in the second phase by the expulsion of women and children. They were driven into the desert, deprived of food and water, and subjected to rape and random slaughter. They endured what for many of them became a Death March.

My grandfather was one of the men who were executed in that first phase. His wife, my grandmother, later took my mom on the second-phase death march. An estimated 100,000 women and children made that trek. Nobody can even guess how many of them died along the trail.

The genocide was the final step in centuries of Turkish abuse. The people in the dominant culture regarded Armenians as dogs and pigs. A Turk would become outraged if the mere shadow of a passing Armenian touched any part of his person. For centuries, Armenians endured outrageous insults and periodic acts of random unprovoked violence against their properties and their very lives. Turkish courts would not admit the testimony of an Armenian against a Muslim. The law forbid them to carry weapons, ride a horse, build

A Life of Miracles

a house that was situated on a higher elevation than the house of a Muslim, or to ring church bells. Any transgression of these oppressive laws called for severe punishment or even execution.

My mother was born into that society. Her father was a member of a prominent family in Kharp, Turkey. Grandpa was an educated person and a respected member of the community. Mom was the youngest of eight children and the only girl. Her mother, my grandmother, was a woman of prayer and faith who passed her life of devotion down to her children. The Bible said that the blessings of devout parents would be passed down to "the third and fourth generation," and I guess that happened in my case, because the dynamic faith of those two women found a welcome home in my own spirit.

Even though my grandparents were upstanding members of the community—admired and honored by their neighbors—they were Armenians and therefore caught up in the killings. The executions began with community leaders and members of the educated intelligentsia. My father was the sort of good and upstanding person that they wanted to kill first.

Ani Amoore

My mother got caught up in the horror when she was 12 years old. It began when neighbors and friends were taken from their homes and summarily executed in nearby fields. So when soldiers came to their door one day and asked for my grandfather's whereabouts, Grandmother told them that he was not home. They grabbed my mother and said, "If you do not get him for us, we will torture the little girl." When Grandpa heard that, he came out of hiding. "Here I am," he said. They took him to a nearby field, together with a number of men from the town, and shot them all as though they were diseased animals.

Our family's Turkish neighbors, who had admired my father and liked our family, told my mother the details of how my grandfather died. We learned that Grandpa survived the initial wound. So they shot him a second time, but even then Grandpa was still alive. There was apparently some standard among those horrible people that they should release any victim who survived more than two gunshots. Perhaps this was a superstition, but at any rate some of the others apparently suspected that they were witnessing a miracle and told the shooter to stop. However, he shot him a third time and Grandpa died there in the field.

When soldiers later drove them out of their homes in the second phase, my mother and grandmother set off

A Life of Miracles

on foot with a number of other women and struck out through the desert of Deir ez-Zor. My mother was with one of a dozen children traveling with a group. There endured horrible things—so bad that I put them out of my memory. The women and children cooked grass, ate dead birds, and drank water out of puddles. The Turkish soldiers who guarded them often raped the pitiful and helpless walkers.

At one point on that long march, one of the guards picked my mother up and carried her to a remote area where he was going to molest her. At that point, Mom experienced the first of what would become many miracles. "Jesus, help me," she cried out. The rapist began shouting, "You bloody Christian. You are nothing but a barbarian!" She again began crying out to God and suddenly God filled her with strength, as He had Sampson, and she pushed the man down to the ground. He cursed at her but was not able to get up and pursue her again. She was able to return to the other women and to relative safety.

Every day some of the women would collapse and die along the trail. Sometimes the soldiers would put them out of their misery by shooting them, as they would a rabid dog. When they came to the Euphrates River, many of the shorter women were not able to keep their footing, so they were carried down stream by the current and drowned. It was a pitiful spectacle, made even more horrible by the fact that some of the women had been carrying infant children who joined them in their watery grave.

My grandmother had been growing weaker and finally, after crossing the river, she collapsed and died in my mother's arms. They had taken refuge in an inn that, as it turned out, belonged to a secret Armenian who had been passing as a Turk. Grandma's final words were ones of love and concluded with an admonishment to her young daughter to keep walking and to never stop until she got to safety. The innkeeper helped my mother to dispose of Grandma's body and then Mom set out on the trail alone.

Years later Mom told me that the memory of her holding Grandma in her arms and watching her take her final breath was one that throughout her life continued to haunt her nighttime dreams and daytime memories.

Mom and the others who survived the Death March arrived in Aleppo where they discovered that World War I had ended. Even more wonderful, on a personal level, was her discovery that two of her brothers had survived the massacre. One had moved to Egypt, but the other lived in Aleppo. She learned the address and arrived at his house with her clothing in rags and body emaciated to the point of starvation. Her brother was on some errand and the house was empty. When she detected the heavenly aroma of dolmas cooking in the neighbors' kitchen, her hunger overtook her so she snuck into the neighbors' house, stole a dolma, and ate it. When the woman returned, Mom confessed her crime, but the woman noted my mom's condition, told her she had done the right thing, and actually gave her some more dolmas.

After all the horrors of that trip (and I haven't told you some of the worst), that incident in the kitchen was one of the few things from the tragedy that brought smiles to us throughout the intervening years.

While Mom was living with her brother, my father came from his St. Louis home in order to be with his parents, who lived in Turkey. Dad brought with him a thousand dollars, which was a lot of money at that time, to invest in starting a business. Unfortunately, his timing was bad since he arrived during the massacre. Perhaps because of the relative wealth he was carrying, the Turks didn't kill him, but they confiscated the money. He got a job in a restaurant located in a fine hotel, made famous by the fact that Churchill made it his habit to stay there when he was in Turkey. Dad was able to get the position of *maitre'd* because, after living in Missouri, he was able to speak good English.

Dad and Mom met, fell in love, married, and had their first child—my older sister, Varsen, who lived until 2010 when she died at the ripe old age of 89 years. Mom later gave birth to two sons.

My father moved his young family to Jordan where he had some cousins who owned a successful restaurant. Because of Dad's command of English, he got a fine position in the establishment. Life was good. But even though his cousins begged him to stay, before long he decided that he wouldn't remain in Jordan. Father's ambition was to move to America and Jordan had no American consulate, so he moved back to Turkey and they immigrated to St. Louis, where they opened a bakery that specialized in delicious pita.

My Father loved his life in America, but in the meantime his parents had opened a successful restaurant in Egypt, and they persuaded him to come to them and work in the family business. So he moved his family to Egypt where a terrible tragedy overtook him. His two sons, my brothers, who were brilliant happy children, both died of disease. One was 12 years old and the other was just six. In later years, when they spoke about my two brothers, people would recall that both had beautiful blue eyes.

A Life of Miracles

My mother never completely recovered and years later, when she spoke to me about the heartbreaking loss, she added, "I should have died then, myself." Dad never recovered either. Following the death of the children, he was overcome by grief and was no longer willing to live in a place with such gloomy associations, so they moved, with my sister, to Cyprus, and moved in with some relatives.

CHAPTER 2

MY CYPRIOT CHILDHOOD

Cyprus turned out to be a barren land for my parents. The people at that time were backwards and the economy impoverished. Residents didn't go out to eat, so my father's attempts failed to replicate the success with his restaurant that he had enjoyed in Egypt and St. Louis. He invested his money in a house that turned out to be a scam, so he and Mom became nearly destitute. To make the tale of their calamity final, Dad contracted cancer.

Then I was born.

When I learned about the wilderness experience that my parents had been going through during my birth, I asked my mother why she had ever given birth to me. Mom told me that before her pregnancy, a prophecy had been given about my birth. When she told me the story, Mom said that a vision had come to her that she was going to have a little girl who was destined to become a blessing to the members of her family and to a great host of people. "You are going to be a special little girl," she told me.

My first dramatic answer to prayer occurred when I was 13 years old and attending school in Cyprus. A girl named Lucy was the undisputed leader of our little society. She was a bully who would favor the girls who followed her leadership and would push out of the circle anyone who went contrary to her wishes. The other girls then avoided contact with the outcast, who would thus become ostracized and isolated from the group.

One day Lucy asked me to give her a ride home on a new bicycle that Mom had made great sacrifice to purchase. I declined, telling Lucy that I was afraid of falling down and damaging my new bike. She took the rejection personally and told me that I knew what was going to happen to me starting the next day. She made good on the threat and from that point on made my life in school a real misery. I tried to tell Mom about the awful thing that was happening to me, but couldn't make her understand how dreadful my life had become. I attempted to make things right with Lucy, but when I went to her house to speak with her, she shut herself in a closet so that she wouldn't be able to listen to even one word from me.

I began to learn the truth of the words from an old

A Life of Miracles

gospel song, "No one ever cared for me like Jesus." When I went to Him in prayer, I sensed that He met me in my loneliness. I was aware that He was present with empathy and understanding.

Things didn't get any better at school, so I finally decided to stage a spiritual showdown. I reasoned that if God really was a father to me. He would understand and give me the help that I needed.

"Dear God," I prayed, "If you really are listening, make Lucy stop; make her talk to me tomorrow."

The very next day when I got to school Lucy came up to me in a friendly manner. She game me a hug, "Let's talk!" she said. Her abrupt change of attitude would have been baffling except I knew that the One who could change hearts had intervened to change hers.

Perhaps the prayer represented a real turning point in my life. The life of faith I had already been leading might have come to a grinding halt if God hadn't answered that simple prayer. However, on that day I learned that the loving presence of a powerful God was a dependable reality. Faith had become more than simple belief or philosophy; it had become grounded true knowledge, and actual reality, based upon undeniable experience.

When I got home, I knelt down in gratitude and

worship. At that moment I became a genuine follower of Jesus Christ.

I've come to realize that God really did give me a special ability, which was to be for people what they need. If they were straying, I would direct them in the right path. If anxious, I would help them to find peace. If they were searching for a life partner, I would help them find the right spouse. In every case, I tried to impress them with the fact that I was no saint or miracle worker, but was simply a channel through which the love and power of God could flow into the lives of others. Jesus Christ was the Good Shepherd who would lead them, heal them, and give them peace.

"God will answer prayer," I told them, "and then you will know that Jesus is alive and listens and provides." As often as I could, I would use the story of my own life as encouragement. "He will lead you and provide for you as He did for me," I would tell them.

Much later, I learned that the truth of the vision was a little more complicated than Mom remembered. During those sad days in Cyprus, Mom had been a member of a prayer circle. One of the members, Mom's best friend, was an Armenian lady from a prominent family. One day, years later we were visiting people in Cyprus and learned that the woman's daughter-in-law was ill. Even though the daughter-in-law's condition was desperate, she called me to her bedroom. "I'm the one who saw the vision," she told me. Then she said that the same vision had come to her on three separate occasions before my mother's pregnancy. She said that Mom had been depressed and distraught. When she first told her of the vision, Mom said, "We have no money! My husband is dying! This pregnancy is ridiculous!"

The woman's account of her three visions encouraged my mother to welcome my birth as a gift from God and by the time she was able to talk about my birth, Mom imagined that she had been the one that had the vision.

"I saw the vision exactly as I am telling you," the woman told me. "Now it's up to you what you will with the information." She died a few months later, as though God had kept her alive until she could tell me the story.

Father's reaction to the news of my impending arrival on earth was far different than Mom's. After I was born, he was delighted with me. "I have a beautiful girl," he told my mother. There was sadness, of course, because he knew that his cancer was terminal. My sister told me that he would hold me in his arms and lament that he wouldn't see me grow up. He died when I was two years old and my sister was 20. My sister was an intelligent woman. She quit school, worked as a seamstress, and would bring home the little bit of money she made to help with our finances. She and mom would take turns caring for me.

My father died before my earliest memories, but it was difficult for me as a young girl to cope with his absence. Sigmund Freud was right when he said that he could not think of any need in childhood as strong as the need for a father's protection. I would sit on men's laps when they would come to our house. However, prayer brought the presence of God into my life and He brought healing for that terrible wound. In the absence of my earthly parent, I discovered that God was not simply a father in heaven but also a dad at my side. He loved me and desired only the best for me.

My earliest memories are of that little Cyprus home. I began attending school when I was five years old and lived in Cyprus until I was 18. In spite of the fact that we were poor, mine was a wonderful childhood. Mom worked long hours so I hardly saw her. I attended an American school where I got a good education and learned to speak English. In the evenings I would miss my mother so much that I would go to meet her and wait for her to come out of work so we could walk home together.

My sister Varsen got married and the lack of a father figure was partially offset by the arrival of my brother-in-law, Kaspar, who came to the house to live with us. He was a good person. He wasn't able to take the place of my missing dad, but it was nice to have him around.

When I was six years old, my niece was born. Mom had mid-wife at the birth of all my sister's children. I was six years old when the first baby came. "Why is Varsen crying?" I asked. She had three more children, and Mom was by her side at each delivery.

My mother was my great example of living life in the presence of God. She was a woman of prayer. Each morning she would begin her day at 5:00 a.m. by getting on her knees. As soon as I was old enough to imitate her, I began praying with her, even though I had no idea what I was doing.

"Who wakes you up?" I asked her one day.

"God does."

Things changed in my life. "In all your ways acknowledge him and he will direct your paths," the Bible says. I admit that I am not perfect. Sometimes

Ani Amoore

I have failed to "acknowledge Him" with disastrous results, but I always find my way back. After all, if a sparrow doesn't fall to the ground without Him knowing, He will certainly lift me up when I have fallen and will care for me.

My family is connected to a genuine superstar. For years my grandmother would meet and pray with another lady—the grandmother of Garo Yepremian—an NFL kicker who, during a 15 year career played for four professional teams, especially the Miami Dolphins. Garo was born and raised in Cyprus and we knew each other as children. Garo's grandmother and mine would pray together twice a week. I would sit off to the side and watch them as they read the Bible and was impressed with how they prayed together fervently and with great faith. In those days, however, Garo himself was something of a pest. He often behaved in such a naughty fashion that I would grow angry with him and would shout at him, "I'm going to beat you" and then chase him out of the front door with a stick.

Years later, when he was a big star, Garo and my nephew would hang out in Oakland between games. Sometimes Garo would come around to visit. He would tease me. "You can't beat me now," he would say. He laughed and bragged about how he had become so famous. "I'm more famous than you," he said. That made us laugh, since how famous would you have to be to be more famous than I was?

Garo once told me that his grandmother had provided him with the greatest example of godliness and faith. She was a wonderful woman—one who probably provided a wonderful example for many other people.

When I was eight years old, Mom developed a case of elephantitis. It was a horrible, disfiguring, and deadly disease. I knew she was ill, but didn't know how desperate her situation was. I left her for a short time one day to attend choir practice at our little church. A girl came in and said they should begin tolling the church bells because someone was dying. They didn't say any name but I knew instantly that it was my mother for whom they were planning to ring the death knell, so I ran home as fast as my legs could carry me.

I arrived to discover the priest giving her last rites. She gave the appearance of someone obviously dying.

The priest and her doctor left because they knew her case was hopeless. I ran outside and prayed desperately, crying out to God. When I reentered the house, Mom called me over to her side and told me in a clear voice, "Don't tell anyone else, but Jesus has healed me. I'll be walking in a few days. Don't cry any more." Her face was shining as though illuminated by a beam from heaven. The swelling went down and before long she returned to work. Jesus had performed a miracle in her body just like the miracles of healing He performed during His ministry.

Mom was always generous. Even though we were in poverty ourselves, she would give things away to the poor. Sometimes I would question her, "Why are you giving that away?" She would always answer, "They need it more than we do." That seemed to be her main criteria. Mom had no money to contribute to the church so she would clean the church building every week instead of giving a monetary offering.

Nobody lives forever. A number of years after her amazing healing, the doctors told Mom that she needed surgery. My sister and I advised her against having an operation. What Mom didn't share with us was that she had cancer. For the next decade, she fought against the disease. I would see her suffering and would think each day she was going to die. She was confined to her bed at the end. My sister and I were sitting together near her. We knew that the end was approaching.

Mom had not been taking morphine; her mind was clear. Suddenly the room filled with light and a big smile came over our mom's face. "Did you see what I saw?" she asked. "The Virgin was here; she brought my two sons with her. They were so beautiful. They were holding three candles. The Virgin told me, 'In three days you are going to come home.'"

During those three days, I was grieving, even though I wondered if it had been a true vision. On the third day, Mom told me that she didn't mind dying; she was concerned about me. She said that she had an out of body experience during which she was taken to heaven. Mom later shared with me the events that transpired during her near-death experience. She had the sensation of being lifted up higher and higher. Then she described the heavenly beauty that filled her eyes. She said rows of angels were standing on both sides of her. "They were calling me blessed," she said. Mom said furthermore that her ears were filled with heavenly songs that she could only describe as "the music of the spheres." A vision of beauty and color.

My brother-in-law, Kaspar, said that at the time the

sight of doves going up and down above my mom had frightened him. Mom asked him what he was seeing. When he told her, she said, "You have a clean heart. Those are angels who have been helping me and strengthening me and comforting me in my hour of death."

Kaspar told me the story afterwards with tears in his eyes. He said that Mom also told him to take care of me for a year. After that I could go by myself. The angels had told her that I would be cared for. She told me that I had a purpose to show love to others. Mom also blessed Kaspar. "May you walk always with God and love Him," she said. "I bless you financially in every way. May God give you long life and joy and happiness with your children."

On the third day, I reluctantly went to work. I didn't want to go, but on the other hand, I wasn't willing to accept the possibility of my mother's death. At 2:00 p.m. I was talking with my girl friend. I was laughing when I suddenly stopped because I felt my mother's presence near me.

"What happened?" my friend asked.

"I do not know. Something sad has happened." I knew in my heart that Mom was gone. That momentary awareness of her presence that I had experienced was her dear spirit passing me briefly on her way back to the

God whom she had loved and served. Her departure left a vacancy in my heart that has never been filled.

Mom was always full of faith. Especially following her near-death experience with elephantitis when she was taken to heaven and saw the face of Jesus, she never had any fear of death. Just before her passing, she had another out-of-body experience and saw angels singing an anthem of praise that seemed to wrap itself around the world. She died in joyful anticipation. She was only 67 years of age.

Even though Mom had greeted death as "a welcomed friend," her passing left me with feelings of loss and abandonment. I wept uncontrollably. However the day following her death, Mom appeared to my older sister, Varsen. She was shocked "You're dead, Mom!" she said. "We buried you." Varsen told me later that Mom's appearance was transformed. She looked beautiful and young.

Mom told Varsen, "Ani is crying too much. You must tell her that she should stop weeping because I am at peace. My pains are gone. Tell Ani that the two of you should care for each other." Then she said, "I have to go now…."

Varsen said that before she left, Mom walked to the dining table carrying a box with two loaves of bread and placed one on the table. That single loaf of bread left behind made Varsen confused. "I think it means that one of us is going to die," she said. "The meaning is that death will soon take one of us and the other will remain behind."

Varsen and I were close. We loved each other so much that we didn't want either of us to die. The next day Mom came back again and appeared again to Varsen. "I know you are afraid one of you will die," she said. But that's not the point. It simply means that in one year, Ani will be moving out of the house; you will stay here."

Death remains a mystery, of course. But somehow, following her death, Mom knew to comfort me with the true knowledge that I would not remain alone; that someone would come and take me away, which was an obvious reference to my marriage to the man who would become my husband. She further knew that my sister and I had been confused by the symbol of the two loaves of bread and had come back one last time to correct the confusion.

I still think about my dear mother, so many years after her passing. Looking back over my life, which

A Life of Miracles

has been blessed in so many ways, I realize that no memories seem happier than my recollection of sitting in a field with my mother and counting the stars.

John and Ani Amoore

CHAPTER 3

A Love Story

I've learned that life is best when we put ourselves into God's hand. We simply choose His way and thus put ourselves in the way of His blessings. From early childhood, I always prayed that God would prevent me from falling into love with and marrying anybody except the life partner that He would provide for me. Some modern young people seem anxious to get married and will marry the first person they meet, since they are frightened by the prospect of perhaps ending up a bachelor or old maid.

However, I believed that if I would just wait on God, He would provide me with a true soul mate. As a result, I married the best man I ever met. From the beginning of our relationship until he took his final breath, John Amoore was always kind, loving, and respectful. He treated me like I was a queen, and I thought of him as an angel come down from heaven. The two of us lived in wedded bliss and in happy service for God and man until John's death, two decades ago, following 35 years of marriage.

I had several opportunities to marry the wrong man before I met John. In those days, I was not lacking for suitors, and a number of young men came into my life who were interested in dating me. They would come to see Mom in order to ask for my hand in marriage. In each case, I would take it to God in prayer, and ask, "Is this man for me?" And in every case God would answer "No." One in particular was a beautiful person and seemed like he would be a perfect mate for me. I would have been glad to accept the man's affections and prayed that God would show me that he was the one. However, I suddenly felt that he was, in fact, not the one, so I broke off relationships with him.

I was perfectly confident that when the right man would eventually come along, I would be given the unmistakable sign that he was Mr. Right. Mom turned out to be more attracted to my suitors than I was. She wanted me to get married so she could witness my wedding and see some grandkids.

The economic situation in our little family improved when jobs suddenly became available to people who were educated and could speak English. I passed the entrance exam and got a job working at an ordinance depot in Dhekelia Cantonment, which is the official British Overseas Territory on our little island. I was an administrative assistant; John Amoore was my boss. The British were running things and John was the head of the office where I worked.

The first time I saw John, it seemed that God was giving me the sign I had been waiting for, and I felt certain that he would become my husband. The conviction wasn't logical because, on the surface, there didn't seem any possibility of a marital alliance between John and me. Mom was in the first stages of what would be her final illness, and I was supposed to marry an Armenian.

Far more difficult was the fact that John occupied a place in society far above my own. The social norms in Cyprus in those days were different than in contemporary England. In particular, the British society we moved in was highly organized by class and, as a member of a fine British family, a graduate student at the University of Oxford, and my boss, John moved in circles higher than my own. However, destiny will not be denied, and much later John shared with me that he had gotten the same message about me that I had received about him. He once pointed me out to some of his friends. "I like the shy one," he said.

A warm friendship sprang up between the two of us. Even though we had never gone on a date, John began to visit with me every day in the office. One day he asked if he could come to see my mother. I was reluctant for the two of us to be together without a chaperone, so he said he would bring a friend with him. I asked permission from my mom to bring my boss to meet her. When John showed up at our house with his friend, Mom took an instant liking to him. She had pictured him as a much older man.

John and I began to see each other socially. On one unforgettable occasion, he actually invited me to attend a dance at the officers' club. Of course, we were chaperoned, which was the only proper conduct, in those days. On three occasions, he and his friend would come visit me in my house. He was in love with me—a relationship made easier by the fact that mom had also come to love him.

While preparing for death, Mom had an out-of-body experience. Even though John and I were not in any relationship at that time, she returned from her Celestial Visit with the conviction that John and I were to marry. She gave me the instructions, "When he asks you to marry him, say yes." I believe she must have gotten some foresight during her time in heaven so that she could die in the happy knowledge that I would be safely married.

A Life of Miracles

John and I continued seeing each other, but our growing association came to an abrupt and lengthy detour when he announced that he was returning to Oxford to complete his doctorate. After he left I wept inconsolably. I continued working but with a different attitude about the job. I was feeling gloomy with sad thoughts about my absent love. We began writing occasional letters to each other, and he said nice things about missing my smile and the pleasure of my company. We had no understanding between us; our relationship was not exclusive. However, John volunteered the reassuring information that whenever he would go on a date with somebody, the date would never amount to anything because my face would continually flash before his eyes.

My mother passed while John was in England, but her prophecy from beyond the grave began to take place shortly after her passing when my cousin, Garbis, a professional musician, bought a house in England. He contacted me. "Your mom just died," he said. "Why don't you come visit?" I prayed about it and decided to make the trip.

My sister couldn't believe that I was going and nobody, including myself, thought it would turn out to be anything special. This was long before email and other social media, of course. I had written "snail mail" letters to inform John and other people in England about my arrival. I never heard back from him and wondered what had become of my suitor. I never expected to see him again.

I had a nice visit with my cousin and on the day I was scheduled to return to Cyprus John showed up. It turned out that he had been on vacation with some friends from Australia and finally read my letter just in time. He told me later that when he learned of my presence in the country he began to jump up and down. His friend and major professor, Hans Krebs, a leading scientist and inventor of the Krebs Cycle, was alarmed by the sight of John suddenly leaping about. "Are you going crazy?" he asked.

"The girl I love is right here!" John replied.

The next day he came to my cousin's house where I had been staying. Society was more relaxed in England than in Cyprus, so the two of us were at last able to go on a date without a chaperon looking over our shoulder.

"I don't want you to go back to Cyprus," John said.

A Life of Miracles

"I am going to take you to see my mother." At that first meeting, John's Mom turned out to be less loving of me than my mom had been of John. She didn't like the fact that I was an Armenian girl. After all, how could an Armenian girl marry an Oxford scholar? The answer was based upon the reality that, as Jesus said, "With God all things are possible."

Years later, John's mom admitted that she actually didn't want her son to be married at all. She was a Cambridge bred scientist and had accomplished the extraordinary feat, for those days, of being a female department head and managing a team of 300 people involved in physics research projects. She lived in a place called Monmouth Shire, which was on the border of Wales and England, so John and I would occasionally take the 12-hour driving trip to visit her.

John's mom was a graduate of Cambridge so she and her son would have some merry disputes about which university was the better. She would also explain things to us, such as how scientists were able to compute the exact distance to the moon.

John's aunt, Dr. Brenda Winterton, was a surgeon. Her father was one of the leading accountants in England and actually managed some of the accounts for the Royal household. Dr. Winterton belonged to a learned society and on one unforgettable occasion took us as her guests to hear a speech by a renowned scientist.

I also met Dr. Anna Bidder, John's godmother, who was a close friend of the family and a noted marine biologist who specialized in jellyfish and had worked with Jacque Cousteau. Dr. Bidder told me a great story about her father. He lived in Naples and was a resident of Palmer's Hotel. He would work at night and sleep during the day. He was very strict about not wanting anyone to awaken him. He was wealthy so they followed his orders. However, one day he heard a persistent knocking at his door. "Dr. Bidder can you get up?"

"Why should I get up?"

"People who are interested in buying the hotel want to see your room."

"Go away," he said. "And I'll buy the hotel myself."

John and I visited the hotel and learned that the story was true.

John's elderly Aunt Mae was a lovely woman, but experiencing dementia, forgetting everything, and making such mistakes as paying some bills twice. I invited her to spend a month with us. One day John discovered that Aunt Mae had been hoarding food beneath her bed. When he remonstrated with her, she explained, "These people do not feed me."

Our landlady once saw Auntie Mae walking about in the middle of the night.

"Where are you going, Auntie Mae?" she asked.

"I am going back to London," she replied. "I am going home."

In spite of her failing mind and body, I enjoyed those days with Auntie Mae. I would bathe her and hold her frail body in my arms.

John refused to let me return to Cyprus. He sealed our future together by giving me a ring. I almost called off the wedding because John had become an agnostic. He would pray with me, but one day I asked him, "Are you a committed Christian?"

"I used to love God," he answered. "And I loved to read the Bible, but Mom is an agnostic and after I went to Oxford, I decided she was right. I became an agnostic, as well." The fact is, John's mom was a little shaken in her agnosticism. She told me once that she envied my faith.

I had always imagined I would not give my heart

away to a person who lacked personal faith in God, so I told John I would wait a week before responding to his proposal. I needed to pray about the decision. While I was praying God came to me in a very real and undeniable way and told me very clearly, "Take him. He's mine." So after the seven days were up, I told John that I would marry him.

Following our marriage, John met some good people in Edinburgh, attended a Bible study, and finally made a decision to give his life to God. I realized that God doesn't leave you alone; once you commit yourself to Him, if you are truly sincere in your heart, as John always was, God will bring you back. An old hymn spoke the truth in the words, "Love found a way to redeem my soul." At that point, John and I began praying together regularly and earnestly. That's when the miracles really started to happen.

While we were planning our wedding, John received his doctorate from Queens College, at the University of Oxford. The investiture ceremony took us on a trip back through time. Queen's College was founded in 1341 and the college is located in a set of extravagant and baroque buildings that were completed four centuries before America won its independence from England. The buildings are situated around a Front Quad, which is acknowledged to be Oxford's grandest piece of classical architecture. The ceremony was held in a beautiful venue, the Church of England Kensington.

During the ceremony, John was arrayed in what seemed formal medieval style ceremonial regalia, complete with gown, hood, and bonnet. It was like a scene from some movie about knighthood; they actually tapped him on both shoulders with a sword. It was a great moment, and I was proud of my fiancé and happy with his triumph.

Few of my family were present at the wedding but I had a number of childhood friends. Thankfully, John's family, including his mom, all showed up. Part of the reason for the family eventually accepting me was that John's father had the same kind of immediate and warm affection for me at our first meeting that my mom had for John when they first met.

John and I were married in London at the St. Sarkis Armenian Church, in June 6, 1957. I was sad because few of my family attended. Furthermore, a hairdresser destroyed my hair. However, I met Jeannie, a beautiful

British girl who did my lovely wedding dress. I had a friend in London from Cyprus, named Loretta. The two of us had been schoolmates. When I was getting married, she wanted to help me and be my maid of honor. By the way, Loretta had the distinction that at one time she had a brief conversation with Prince Philip.

My cousin Garbis, with whom I was staying, paid a lovely tribute to my parents during the wedding service. He told how when he was a child, his grandfather, a priest, beat him and he would come to my folks for refuge. His speech was poignant and filled with love; Mom would have loved it.

Throughout the years of my marriage I continued to follow my main intention and purpose in life, which was to serve others. I followed the Lord's leading through the changing locations as my husband's work as a scientist in the Food industry led on a winding path through Japan, Hong Kong, and Europe.

Following graduation from his doctoral program, a famous biochemist offered John a research position based on his work in support of the theory of chemical olfaction and the cancer research he had conducted on Rat Liver Mitochondria. John wrote a scholarly article, "The Permeability of Isolated Rat-liver Mitochondria to Sucrose, Sodium Chloride and Potassium Chloride at 0" that is still referenced by ongoing research in the field.

A Life of Miracles

The scientist met with John two days before he was scheduled to go back to Cyprus. "I enjoyed reading your papers," he said. "But I expected a much older man." He offered John a research position at the university and my life in Cyprus came to an abrupt end.

The opening years of married life had a dream-like quality. John and I took up life in Edinburgh. He easily fit into the University life because John's professor at Edinburgh, Dr. Brown, who had formerly been in Oxford at Queen's College, moved to Edinburgh at the same time John did.

Six months after we were married, John's parents gave us their honeymoon car—a 1938 Ford Princess. John loved the old car. It had leather upholstery. We began attending a Baptist Church that was served by a minister and wife who were a wonderful couple. The members were friendly and kind and would often invite us home for dinner following Sunday worship.

We rented an apartment in a beautiful building that had formerly been a manor house. The fine home had been divided into four apartments, each of them occupied by a professor. The landlady was a wealthy woman named Elizabeth Ferrar. The home was in an upscale part of the city and was surrounded by residences owned by members of Edinburgh's most elite social circles.

It was a beautiful home, situated on the edge of one of Scotland's famous golf courses, so we would occasionally find golf balls lying around in the garden paths and lawns around the place. I asked Elizabeth one day if she wasn't annoyed by the golf balls that would come sailing onto the property. She said she didn't care about them because they didn't come very often, and the beautiful situation by the golf course was worth the annoyance of an occasional golf ball bouncing into the yard. I told her that I would never permit it because bothered me so much. (I eventually got over it. I now live on a golf course, myself, and find golf balls in my yard all the time.)

Elizabeth wrote mystery novels and was a friend of Agatha Christie, so I would go from room-to-room to see if anything mysterious might be lurking in the corners of that fine old house. I never found anything.

John and I were the only couple in residence and Elizabeth waited on us like we were upstairs residents at Downton Abbey. She and I would sit together for hours and talk. For six months, I never had to cook. We would partake of high teas and formal meals eaten with silver service and conducted like small theatrical productions.

A Life of Miracles

The meals were as entertaining as they were nutritious.

The four years we spent at the university was a golden period in my life. Edinburgh was beautiful and seemed to be a cultural resource for that part of Great Britain. Numerous festivals and playhouses in the area served as testing grounds for new productions. If the citizens of Edinburgh liked a play, it would go on to open in London.

Through his contacts at the school, John was able to get two theater tickets for the price of one, and the two of us would regularly attend some play or performance. Elizabeth and I also had a shared affection for the theater and had season tickets to a major venue. Every week the two of us could be found sitting in the front row at one performance or another. We especially enjoyed the annual Edinburgh Festival that was a destination for people from all over the world.

When January 25 came around, we attended the annual Burns Night event, during which they read from the works of Robert Burns. I was appalled by the obscene language and vulgar stories that were laughingly read to us. My face was red down to my neck. All the ladies who were present were blushing furiously throughout the whole reading. I'm sure that's true, because any female who could listen to that without blushing would be no lady.

Ani Amoore

My Cypriot-based sensibilities were dazzled by the refined society that I suddenly found myself a part of. I was blessed with a good husband, friends who loved me, and a residence in an English manor house. I never took it for granted; I was grateful every day for being surrounded with such beauty and by people whom I loved and who loved me.

During our time in Edinburgh, I also became special friends with a Colombian debutante named Fanny, whose parents had served at the Colombian Consulate. She hated the ritual, ceremony, and pomp associated with her parents' lives, so she fled the consulate and never returned. She lived for a while with John and me. If the subject of her defection would come up, she would say, "I do not want to be a debutante. I am a simple girl." The two of us played tennis together. Whenever she lost, she would swear in Spanish. (I was grateful to not understand the language.)

We only rented with Mrs. Downey for six months and then thought we should have our own place. A few houses down from our apartment was a beautiful home owned by a woman who had lost her husband. She rented us a nice two-bedroom apartment in the upstairs floor.

The location was lovely, adjoining Edinburgh Park. John would walk through the park to get to work and then come home for lunch. Every morning a huge limo would stop by the park and a uniformed man would get out with a small dog. The two of them would walk around the park, get back in the limo, and drive back to wherever they had come from. We never learned who owned the limo. Royalty perhaps.

Elizabeth and I remained great friends and she was sad years later when we moved to America. "Always remember me," she said, and presented me with an ornate jade cup, trimmed in platinum, to help keep her memory alive.

The air around our new home would often be filled with the sound of skirling bagpipes because next door stood a massive and beautiful manor house inhabited by the heirs to the Crabbie's fortune that had been earned by marketing Scottish Whisky in various blends and labels. On the other side, stood a beautiful home inhabited by the owners of the large Scott Lyons Bakery. The Lyons and Crabbies both were wonderful neighbors! It took a while to develop friendships with them, but then they became friends indeed.

We fit in well with the mannered society that we found ourselves part of. One day John saw a man going through our garbage. "Will you kindly put that back when you are done?" The man responded in a beautifully accented voice. "I'm going to my brother's house."

I was dumbfounded. "Scott Lyons is your brother?" I asked.

Later when we spoke with Scott about the incident, he confirmed that the man was his brother indeed, and that he was a college graduate, but simply preferred living a hobo lifestyle.

The Crabbie's Whisky people would invite us for elegant dinners. The family butler would welcome us, sit us at the table, and we would join the entire family in conversation that was always refined and enjoyable while dining on food that was always appealing and tasty.

The matriarch of the family loved painting. She and her three friends wanted to paint me and invited me to their studio. I discovered the studio was a large community affair and was shocked by the sight of naked models posing for their pictures. At first, I shielded my eyes from the nudity, which greatly amused the painters. However, I discovered to my surprise that it took only

A Life of Miracles

a short while to become accustomed to being around naked people. However, I remained fully clothed while my friend painted a beautiful picture of me.

One day I took some guests from Cyprus to see the Crabbie estate home in Northern Scotland. It was locked and we were peering through the window at the beautiful furnishings. Suddenly a man rode up on a horse and screamed at us in a thunderous voice telling us to get out. I recalled that one of the painters said that her husband was the caretaker.

"Are you Dorothy's husband?" I asked. "She's the one who painted my picture." The man suddenly recognized me from the picture, and his attitude changed in an instant from roaring lion to gentle lamb. I learned from the experience not to judge others quickly for any harsh behavior or attitude. There is a lamb somewhere beneath almost every savage lion façade if only we have the patience to search for it.

One of our pleasant and healthy activities during that time was playing tennis with the other young professors. Even though most of the young couples we hung out with during those days were Scottish, they loved Armenian food. I imagine that anyone who can eat haggis should be able to enjoy a good *dolma* or *kufteh*.

We would go on outings and one day planned a picnic to the famous Loch Ness. I had prepared some of my favorite Armenian dishes. We arrived at the loch in a snowstorm. I had worked hard on preparing the food, so I told the others that we weren't going to waste either my efforts or the food so we ate our picnic in the snow. We kept watching for Nessie to poke his monstrous head above the waves, but he never showed. We imagined that he might have been discouraged by the inclement weather.

The fine homes, food, and entertainments in Edinburgh were wonderful, of course, but the springs of true happiness come from our hearts and never from our circumstances. I believe a person can never find joy through fine things who would be unable to be happy without them. There were a lot of unhappy miserable people in Edinburgh.

We loved every part of Edinburgh except the weather. Our house didn't have central heating and the only source of warmth on cold days came from a rented space heater that operated only when we inserted shillings. On brutally cold days, we had to put our feet under the heater in order to thaw out.

A Life of Miracles

Each winter, John and I would leave the dank and dismal Scottish climate behind and spend a month, or so, traveling on the continent. One year we started in Belgium and drove the whole length of Europe. We didn't have much money so we stayed in hostels, enjoying the company of the happy carefree students from around the world and especially from America.

Our route took us through all the European cultural centers, stopping at cathedrals and museums. Every part of the trip was grand, but I particularly fell in love with Austria, and in particular enjoyed the incredible Schönbrunn Palace that for centuries had been the home for generations of members of the Hapsburg Dynasty. The authentically furnished rooms where the Imperial Family lived and the garden labyrinths had been perfectly restored and maintained. We visited a huge performance hall where the crème of society would assemble to hear performances by Chopin, Mozart, and Beethoven.

I have always loved Chopin and in Cyprus would ask my girlfriend, who was an accomplished pianist, to play his music. One unforgettable day while standing in the center of that hall, I experienced a few moments during which I was nearly overwhelmed as some connection was suddenly made between my spirit and scenes from the distant past. I experienced a sense of *déjà vu* so powerful that my husband asked me what was wrong. The fact is that there was nothing wrong. On the contrary, I felt a gentle feeling of complete relaxation and a comfortable impression of being transported to a period of history long before my birth but nevertheless seemed a time in which I felt a sense of belonging. My body was clothed in an elegant old-fashion period dresses and I was dancing to the strains of Chopin and other artists.

The astounding experience only lasted a short time before I was returned to the modern world and found myself once again standing beside my husband in that silent hall.

I don't know what to think of that strange episode. However, I told the story to a close friend who said that she had experienced a similar case of *déjà vu* while standing in that very place.

After four years, John was given a sabbatical. He had visited Cal Tech while working on his undergraduate degree and actually worked on a project with Linus

A LIFE OF MIRACLES

Pauling, one of the Twentieth Century's most important scientists—one of the founders both of Quantum Chemistry and Molecular Biology, and the only person to be awarded two unshared Nobel Prizes.

John had enjoyed wonderful times with his American friends, so he chose Berkeley as the place to spend his sabbatical. At the beginning, I didn't like Berkeley. After the sophisticated culture and elegance of London and Edinburgh, Berkeley seemed like a shabby village. As we drove down University Avenue, my first impressions of the place brought me to tears; I wanted to go home. However, John then took me to San Francisco, and I was impressed with the beautiful City On The Hills. The noisy atmosphere and unique energy of Fisherman's Wharf cheered me up. I loved the crowds of happy people. The place was alive. I decided that I could take a year in Berkeley if we could make regular trips to San Francisco. However, I eventually came to love the campus, the town, and the culture.

Sabbaticals aren't supposed to be vacations, and John spent his time working with a professor who was conducting research on cellular division in mice. John had been working with mice while conducting his research on smell.

While in Berkeley I joined a Bible study fellowship. We moved into a condo and were planning to remain in America for a year and then return to England. We had round trip tickets. However, the course of our lives changed one day when we attended the wedding of an Armenian lawyer in an Armenian Church. It was at the end of the sabbatical period and John and I were preparing to return home in four days. Following the event, we gave a ride to an author named Anne M. Avakian. It turned out she was working for the United State Department of Agriculture (USDA).

"What do you do, John?" Ann asked.

"I am a biochemist," he said.

"I work with biochemists," she said. "I would like to introduce you to some of them." The next day she introduced my husband to a scientist named Dr. John Burr, who was pleased and even excited to meet John. "I've read your papers on the sense of smell," Dr. Burr said. "You seem too young to have written anything that polished and well-done."

As they were talking, Dr. Burr suddenly said, "I want to give you a job. I want you to stay here and finish your work." It was a great opportunity for John because it would give him an opportunity to continue working on the olfactory theory that had caught the attention of the other scientists.

A Life of Miracles

The offer presented us with a problem, however, because we had nearly reached the date at which we had planned to return to Scotland, so we got down on our knees to pray about whether to stay or go. We looked into the Bible for direction and found a verse that seemed exactly to tell us that John and I should remain in California and that he should take up the offer from the USDA lab on the work that, after all, he loved so much.

The weather pushed us over the edge. Mild sunny Northern California had spoiled us. We were reluctant to return to the usually foggy, soggy, and often freezing weather that waited for us in Edinburgh.

We moved out of our condo and bought a house in El Cerrito that was close to his work and was such a perfect place for us to make a home that we felt God had prepared it just for us.

John was happy with his work in the lab. He had discovered that humans are able to detect more than 10,000 separate odors. However, much as the entire spectrum of visible colors and shades result from the combination of three primary colors, John discovered that each of the odors result from combinations of seven primary odors that he identified including sweaty, spermous, fishy, malty, urinous, and musky. The odor of sweat turned out to be an aphrodisiac and the Jovan Perfume Company hired John to be spokesperson for their Musk perfume.

John was thriving and made breakthroughs that earned the attention of the media. He appeared on TV. Magazine articles were written about him. He went on lecture tours all over the world sharing with other scientists his amazing theory. We traveled to Japan during blossom time. The lecture halls were filled with people anxious to hear him speak. He appeared on nationwide Japanese television shows. The Japanese scientists and businessmen loved his theory and put us up in amazing 5-star hotels.

Every romance finally ends in tragedy. My father's death and my mother's illness were horrible experiences, but nothing prepared me for the Valley Of Death that I passed through when my wonderful husband contracted cancer. He struggled with the illness for 17 years. For the first nine years, the two of us suffered in silence before finally sharing it with the kids. It was tough battling the illness, but John was

A Life of Miracles

grateful to God for those years, because they gave him time to watch the children grow up.

Even during his illness, John reached out to others. One morning I was driving to the hospital. I was feeling down and prayed that John would have good news. When I entered the room, John said, "Last night I had a wonderful experience. The man next to me had pancreatic cancer and was crying the whole night. I prayed for him. Suddenly the room was filled with light, the door opened, and Jesus came into the room. He walked to the man and touched him." Then John said, "Jesus came to me, smiled at me, and touched me." That was the sign that lifted my spirits. God answered my prayer.

Jesus healed the man that night. The doctors were amazed by the man's recovery and sent him home with a clean bill of health. John later received a letter from him, writing from his Fresno home. "After your prayer, my healing was complete in a couple days." John and the man exchanged letters for the next ten years, until John passed.

On his deathbed John was taking no morphine or other drugs. He couldn't speak because he was on a respirator. He was lying with his eyes turned towards heaven. All of us noted that he didn't appear to be simply staring into space; his eyes were moving as though he were watching a scene. My daughter, who was standing in front of him, saw that he was staring at something over her right shoulder. His eyes were bright. He was apparently watching someone. Marie could feel the energy. She quietly asked him, "Dad? Can you see something?"

John couldn't answer, so Ronald took his hand. "Dad, if you can see something and it is good, squeeze my hand." John squeezed his hand tightly. He asked if he was seeing departed relatives—naming quite a few loved ones. There was no response. But then Ronald asked, "Do you see Jesus?" I think that might have been the hardest grip of all. For several minutes, all of us remained quietly standing around his bed, simply embracing for as long as possible the sense that we were in the presence of God's Spirit.

Some people might wonder if my husband was having some kind of delirium while he was dying, but I'm convinced he was having a true vision. Other people might wonder what he was seeing, but I know the curtains had parted and John was looking at scenes of heaven. They might wonder who he saw during those final moments, but I know he was looking on the face of Jesus Christ, whom He had loved and served for so many years.

Why should we be surprised by such a thing? The Apostle Paul said that any view we have of heaven now is like looking through a piece of broken glass. But at the end, he said, we will see Jesus "face to face."

From the moment I married John, until he passed away, there was not a single day or a single moment when God wasn't walking through our marriage and our lives with us. The three of us—Jesus, John, and me—somehow still seem to be walking together because I talk to both of them every day.

Even though the days of joy and happiness outnumbered the days of sorrow, like every couple, we passed through some hard places during our lives together. However, every day of our life we walked hand-in-hand with Jesus. There were some places where we slipped and fell, but we never stayed down; we picked ourselves up and got right back on the pathway. We would let go of situations and watch Him open and close doors.

CHAPTER 4

SERVING GOD, FAMILY, AND THE WORLD

I could tell more stories about how God has taken care of me than I could ever fit into this small volume. Life has had a lot of ups-and-downs, blessings and heartaches, happiness and suffering. But through it all, I've been confident that what God has spoken into my life will come to pass, and that He has a purpose in every event and each circumstance. We go through dry periods but then our cup runs over.

Even when people would hurt me and wound me with some thoughtless comment or action, I would hand the harm into the hands of God and would not let my love for the person be altered. After all, in most cases people don't intend to be hurtful. It diminishes us ever to be offended when the other person didn't mean to offend. For that matter, it doesn't make sense to allow ourselves to be offended by insults even when they are intended. After all, why would we permit the actions and behaviors of others to overthrow God's will that we lead happy and joyful lives? Our sense of well-being shouldn't depend upon others treating us with respect. Any sense of entitlement blocks the possibility of perfect happiness.

I didn't want to ever have children because of a childhood memory, from when I was six years old, listening through a window to my sister screaming and crying out in pain as she was in the midst of childbirth. I decided at that point that children weren't worth that kind of anguish and I was never going to do that to myself.

After we had been married for seven years, without children, my husband got up one morning and told me a strange story. "I can't understand such a thing," he said, "but at 4:30 someone woke me up. I looked towards you and saw you lying in a brilliant light with two children, a boy and a girl sleeping on each side." John said that he couldn't believe what he was seeing, but even after rubbing his eyes, the vision persisted. Finally, as he watched, the children disappeared.

"I am a scientist," he said. "But I know what I saw. There were two children lying in bed with you."

I didn't know what to think about his strange account

A LIFE OF MIRACLES

and didn't really believe it had been a true vision. I imagined he just had a ridiculous dream.

A woman asked me why I hadn't had children. I freely admitted that I was too frightened by the prospect of the pain associated with childbirth. She told me that my fear was not from God and added, "I am going to pray that the fear will go away."

God eventually answered the woman's prayer because a couple years later, I suddenly realized that the fear was gone. God had taken it away completely. I said to John, "I am not afraid any more." I removed my IUD and got pregnant right away. John wasn't the least surprised when I told him I was pregnant. "I told you," he said. The boy of his vision was born and three years after that the girl. A boy and a girl, just as in the dream. The event reminded me of the story of my mother and the woman in Cyprus who told Mom about her vision of Mom giving birth to me.

As it turned out, my fears about birth pain had been wasted because both of our children were born Caesarian.

Ronald, named after my father-in-law, was born October 4, 1967 at Berkeley's Alta Bates Hospital. He was a precocious child. When he was two years old, it was time to baptize him. Some of my Baptist friends claimed baptism should be reserved only for adults who have made a conscious decision to receive Jesus as their savior. The controversy bothered me, because I wanted to follow God's will in every part of my life, and especially in this part that potentially affected the spiritual well-being of one of my children.

I never prayed for wealth or money but always for healing and especially for direction, so I cried out to God and prayed fervently, "Let me know what I should do." That week at our Bible study, a new presenter spoke about infant baptism and showed the Biblical arguments for it. That was no coincidence! It was an answer from God. The next week, we baptized Ronald as a member of our redemptive community.

God gave a sign showing his approval of our decision to baptize Ronald. My sister Varsen and brother-in-law Kaspar stood up with us during the baptism. As I handed the baby to the priest, Kaspar began crying like a baby. Later he explained to us that as the priest took Ronald into his arms, the child was suddenly bathed in beautiful light and his body seemed to be covered with oil. When Kaspar said that, goose bumps broke out all over my body. Kaspar had obviously been sensitive to spiritual realities that were hidden from our eyes. I guess we shouldn't have been surprised; Kaspar is the one who saw the angels going up and down into heaven at the time of my mother's death.

I could not believe how beautiful Ronald was; he had the same kind face and features as my husband. John held him in His arms and marveled at how much he looked like him. Ronald grew into a good boy and then into a deeply spiritual man. A priest once told me that my son was the most wonderful Sunday School teacher he had ever known.

At one point, Ronald became engaged to a nice Armenian girl. The relationship was getting serious, but I felt that we needed to go back to my roots in Cyprus. During our final week in Cyprus, some friends invited us to accompany them on an overnight cruise across the Eastern Mediterranean to Egypt to see the pyramids.

When we got on the boat, we found space at a table with a young woman and her boyfriend. We learned the girl's name was Ruth. The four of us spoke together for a while. I thought Ruth looked a little downhearted, so I suggested we go up to the boat's dance floor and do karaoke. I sat listening while the young people took turns singing. After a while, Ruth's boyfriend said he was going to retire so Ronald and Ruth continued their conversation.

Following the cruise, Ruth and Ronald remained in touch with each and began texting on a regular basis. Even though they had been together for only that one evening, Ronald and the girl fell helplessly in love. She broke up with her boyfriend and Ronald broke up with his fiancé. I wasn't happy to lose an Armenian as a potential daughter-in-law, but I had felt that God was sending us to Cyprus for a purpose, and bringing these two people together was obviously the purpose He had in mind.

Of course, now I love my daughter-in-law with all my heart—and especially love Isabel, Johnny, and Jojo the three children that she has given birth to.

I have to describe a miracle that occurred on that trip. During my visit in Cyprus with Ronald, I received help from an angel or else my life would have ended. I was swimming with my friends one day at a popular tourist resort while Ronald was waterskiing with his friends. I left my own friends to go swimming by myself. I greeted a Frenchman when I arrived at the otherwise deserted beach and then swam out into the water.

A LIFE OF MIRACLES

Even though I was a normally strong swimmer, I suddenly felt myself sinking beneath the waves. I came up and cried out for help, but nobody heard me, and I was once again pulled beneath the water. I came up again, cried out and sank back down. The third time I came up, I discovered the Frenchman swimming up to me. He helped me back to the beach. If he hadn't been there, I would certainly have drowned and Ronald would have made the sad journey home by himself. Some might think it was a lucky coincidence that the Frenchman "just happened" to be there at the time. But someone told me that Einstein once said that coincidence is simply God's way of remaining anonymous.

Ronald's sister, Marie, was born three years after her brother. An odd thing happened during the first moments of my daughter's life. Just after she was placed in my arms, she opened her eyes and stared intently into my eyes for a long time. It was as though she recognized me and knew who I was.

Marie was a wonderful baby. She was always loving and caring. She shared my husband's kind heart and gentle ways. As a child, Marie had an old soul and spoke to her young friends and even to me with wisdom far beyond her years. She is a gift from God and has a precious diamond-like quality, in my eyes.

Marie was born in January. When it came time to enroll her in school, she should have waited a year but the principal told us that she was so smart that it would be a waste if she didn't join the next class.

As she grew up, Marie loved playing soccer and tennis. She grew into a bright, thoughtful young woman and then into a wise and responsible adult. However, Marie was always a risk taker. She was 16 years old when we were in Europe and took over the responsibility as our personal chauffeur, driving us all over the continent. On one memorable occasion, Marie got caught in a traffic circle and drove all the way around three times before being able to exit. Marie was too good and too wise to ever be overthrown emotionally by such a thing. She has a good sense of humor, and joined us in our laughter that got louder and more uncontrollable every time she started back around the circle yet once again.

Marie graduated from St. Mary College and, thankfully, lives only five minutes from me. She has become a central person in my life. She once shared with me that as a child she never wanted to break the rules because she knew that I trusted her completely to not cross the line.

A Life of Miracles

Not long after John's passing, I shared with Marie how downcast I was. She gave me a hug, sat down at her computer, and searched for a new home for me. I had very specific ideas of the house I wanted. Marie, said, "Let's look at this house, Mom." She took me to tour the property that was located in a gated community in a Country Club. It turned out to be the house I wished for at every point. As we stood together in the little garden, I prayed and in that moment knew in my heart that God had brought the house to me. I'm still living in that house; it is still perfect.

I had to take a trip out of the country and while I was gone Marie fixed up my new home and helped me move in. When my health deteriorated, she remained by my side caring for me and ensuring that I was taking my medicine. She truly has been angel, sent down from God. Loving, thoughtful, and kind.

Marie has a special place in my heart and life. Through my recent illness, she seemed to know what was happening; knew how I was feeling; knew what I needed. We have swapped roles—Marie now cares for me as I once cared for her. She is the wind beneath my wings.

Ani Amoore

Marie has blessed my life with two wonderful grandchildren. Twelve-year-old Kate looks like her mom and has a lot of her mom and me in her. Kate doesn't like to study, just as I didn't like to study. On the other hand, if someone is lonely, Kate will go and sit by her side. Kate's words, thoughts, and ideas sound like they are coming from a mature person. Her 15-year-old brother Alec loves sports, especially baseball. Both children are good people. Their father Harout is a successful businessman, a good man, good husband, and a good father.

John was a member of a small group of smell-and-taste scientists that developed into a tightly knit social group. John and I would often join with the others for a meal in some restaurant, and I enjoyed the company of the other wives. As we shared joys and sorrows together, I would follow the Bible's instruction to "Rejoice with those who rejoice; mourn with those who mourn." I would only share my faith as opportunity to do so would arise. I would never act like a salesman, but would follow St. Peter's instruction:

"In your hearts revere Christ as Lord. Always be prepared to give an answer to everyone who asks you to give the reason for the hope that you have. But do this with gentleness and respect."

A Life of Miracles

It is only reasonable to be gentle and respectful in sharing our faith because, after all, we don't want people from other religious traditions trying to strong sell their particular beliefs to us.

Even though I never tried to convince the other members of the group that they should adopt my philosophies and beliefs, when I would discover that one of them was having trouble with some health issue, for example, or having some relationship conflict or financial crises, I would share with them my own experiences, describing how my faith had gotten me through some situation that was similar to theirs.

By that time, my life had passed through a lot of difficult situations and it seemed that no matter what story they told me, something similar had happened to me. I always believed that the lord gave me words to say, in those situations. I was wise enough never to speak from a point of strength or to evidence the least amount of pride or satisfaction of having survived some ordeal. I simply described how I had found strength and purpose through a similar experience as theirs and would finish the story by describing how God's power had moved in the situation.

I always concluded by noting that nothing is required of us in order to qualify for the gift of His presence. His favor is not available for any price. The only thing required of us is simply to receive the gift by an act of faith. "I am with you always," Jesus said. We only need to believe that He spoke the truth and then to order our lives by that wonderful presence.

One day I was playing tennis with a pastor's wife. She was in the PTA with me, and we were good friends. She asked me to attend a new study that had started as part of the interdenominational Bible Study Fellowship organization. They were looking for a discussion leader—a woman who would be capable of asking the questions from the lessons and then leading the resulting discussions.

The next day I attended the study and met women who were strangers to me and didn't know who I was. However, I must have made a good impression because the very next day they invited me to be a leader. They had been praying for another leader and told me, "The Lord made it clear that you should be one of our leaders." I questioned the decision, "I'm not even a protestant," I said. "I'm Orthodox."

A Life of Miracles

"That doesn't matter at all," they answered. "You love the Lord."

I somewhat reluctantly accepted the role as but then continued leading the group for the next decade. I greatly enjoyed the gatherings, the comradeship, and especially the lessons about faith and love that we learned from the Bible and from each other's experiences.

Life took an unexpected direction one day. I was shopping in San Francisco's Embarcadero with some friends, saw some beautiful jewelry, and was amazed to discover that the jewels were only costume. I was so pleased with how nice the store was and how lovely their products that I felt compelled to go back. I discovered that the store was a franchise. I called the area franchise manager, Ali, who said that it would be nice to have a store in a Walnut Creek. At first, I thought he was Armenian but, as it turned out, he was Persian. Ali and I hit it off. I kept the possibility before me and spent the next two years in prayer, waiting upon the Lord, and wondering if, and when, He would give me a green light to open that business.

When Ronald graduated from school, I shared the business possibility with both him and Marie. The three of us visited the San Francisco franchise and both children got the idea immediately. We had some funds to use as investment capital but, like Gideon in the Old Testament, before we did anything, we put out a fleece to test if this was the will of God. A suitable location had to be available in Walnut Creek or we would take it as red light and would pursue the plan no farther.

I called the franchise manager, Ali, and asked if we could open a Walnut Creek store. He said that ten people had contacted him about the possibility of opening a franchise in Walnut Creek. I was undeterred by this, and told Ali, "If the Lord wants us to open a store, nobody can stop it from happening." A couple days later Ali called us back, "I am going to give it to you," he said.

Our fleece condition was wonderfully fulfilled when we easily located an ideal Walnut Creek location. For the next two decades, we worked that store as a family affair. It was a wonderful experience because we did not regard the business as simply a way of making money, but prayed and worked to make it a testimony of God's love and kindness.

I could fill a second book with stories about what

happened through our store. Elderly women would bring broken jewelry, and Marie would often fix them without cost. Marie and Ronald had welcoming attitudes and regarded customer service as a way of genuinely serving people rather than as a technique for maintaining and increasing our customer base.

The Lord blessed our time in that store. People would come bringing their problems along with their request for jewelry. I would never cut a conversation short unless customers were waiting. In many cases, we would spend an hour or more with a troubled or grieving person, and it would make no difference whether or not it resulted in a sale.

We had some beautiful moments in that store. For example, a couple came in looking at engagement rings. They selected a ring, the man paid for it with his Visa, then knelt down beside the display case, took the woman's hand, put the new ring on her finger, and asked her to marry him. Of course, she said "Yes" with tears shining in her eyes.

A wealthy woman came in wishing to purchase a tennis bracelet for each of her granddaughters. I learned the woman was dying of cancer but was bravely facing the challenge of living to the fullest the dwindling number of days that remained for her. The woman's story moved my heart, and I wanted to do something to pay homage to her courage, so I presented her with a lovely pin. After she passed, one of her daughters came in (wearing her tennis bracelet) and thanked me for the pin I had given to her mother. She said that her mom had been moved by the gift. "She wore the pin all the time," she said.

Lives changed through our little store. People would come in with stories about such things as the divorce they were going through or their child who had recently died. I sometimes wondered why they were telling me such things, but the people felt safe in sharing with us their struggles and tragedies. They were also glad to share their triumphs and successes. Customers would sometimes come in looking like they were at the top of their game; then they would open up and reveal the pain inside. I would speak gently with them and tell them stories of troubles I went through and how God helped me get through them.

God seemed always to show me appropriate ways of adapting my words to help comfort them in their circumstance. Many times the walls of our little jewelry store would ring with sobs and frequently with laughter. Before leaving, the customers would often give us a hug

A Life of Miracles

and a kiss. Whatever their feelings when they came in, they would leave with a smile on their face.

One woman shared the uncomfortable fact that she had recently escaped from a mental institution. "Something led me to come straight here to your store," she said. "I love it here." I believed the woman's story because there was obviously something wrong with her. However, she loved the shapes and sparkles of our jewelry. She was penniless, so I gave her a few small items. Two days later, the woman was back in the store and handing me a little gift. She smiled as she handed it to me, "This is from me to you" she said. I never saw her again, but I continued to pray for her for a long time.

At one point, I would occasionally see a woman dressed in shabby clothes, hanging around our windows, and looking wistfully at the displays. Finally, one day I went outside and brought her in so we could talk together. She shared how much she loved the jewelry. I said to take whatever she wanted and with shining eyes she selected a few small pieces. The Bible said that it is better to give than to receive. Picking out those pieces of jewelry was probably memorable for the poor woman, but I know it became a wonderful memory for me.

Christmas carolers would come and sing for us. At Halloween, John would dress up in a ridiculous costume. On his head he wore a turquois Godzilla with orange teeth in a gaping mouth that would open and close when John pulled a string. He would drop candy from the mouth into the hands of the delighted children.

Sometimes we made money; other days we didn't, but we always made enough to cover overhead and payroll. Profits were never the main point. It was nice for the family to work together. The kids would occasionally fuss about having to go to work, but they always got over it and enjoyed meeting the people.

The Lord blessed our little business and I continue to see people from time-to-time who recall the conversations they had in our store and will show me things they bought from us. We loved them, and they knew that we did.

CHAPTER 5

Answered Prayer and Other Miracles

From childhood and through the decades of my marriage and beyond, I never doubted God's presence. My husband shared my conviction; he and I would never make any decision or attempt to move in any direction without praying for divine guidance. Our prayers were never about money or material goods, but we prayed for His direction and for His help for friends and family with any challenges they were facing.

I have never attempted by my prayers to convince God to perform some act that I thought was right or to give me something merely because I wished for it. I longed to follow in the path that He was walking rather than attempt to get Him to walk with me in some direction that I had chosen for myself. As a result, even though my way was often filled with difficulties, pain, and loss, I was able to taste God's goodness at every point, and especially to see His hand move powerfully in response to my prayers as He supplied some wonderful gift to offset some loss or a spiritual balm to relieve a pain.

Answers to prayer become the real evidence of God's power. We begin with faith, which is a trusting confidence that He is at work, but then God answers prayer in some undeniable way and faith suddenly moves into a new dimension with a new reality. God really is with us! He obviously is moving in our lives!

Ever since His first appearance to me as a child, God has been answering my prayers and providing continual reminders of the fact that He is by my side and acting on my behalf. The settled conviction that God is a real presence is the foundational truth for all my interactions with the world and my relationships with others. I talk to Him and He answers me. He comes to me in dreams and visions, descending from heaven and enclosing me in His loving embrace.

I'm glad to share the truth that if God could be so present and so powerful in the life of a common person like me, He can hold anybody's hand as they walk through life. "Trust in the Lord with all your heart," is the only condition; the one single requirement.

I've told a number of stories already in this book about the ways God miraculously intervened in my life. Here are a few accounts about ways He revealed His power and presence that didn't fit well into the outline.

A LIFE OF MIRACLES

Prayer Led to a "Word" that Transformed a Relationship

My life of prayer and connection with the Source Of All Wisdom & Power has occasionally given me special knowledge beyond normal comprehension. A leader in a Campus Crusade Bible Study group told me that a woman was troubled and wondered if I could speak with her. I took the woman to lunch. She described how her husband had changed. Both of them were lawyers and he had ceased being kind towards her and was often openly critical. The poor woman said that she had come to the end of her patience; she didn't know what to do and was contemplating beginning divorce proceedings.

Somewhere, out of the blue, I gave the woman some advice, "Have him checked for hypoglycemia," I said. It was an amazing thing to say in light of the fact that I have no medical training and didn't even know what the word hypoglycemia meant. Nevertheless, the woman took her husband in for a medical exam, they checked his sugar levels, and discovered that he indeed was hypoglycemic. He was treated for the condition and afterward returned to his normal behavior.

My strange advice might have had an international impact because not long after the event, the man was given an important position under Ronald Reagan.

A Life of Miracles

Answers to Prayer Astonished Japanese Millionaires

While visiting in Japan as part of John's lecture tour, we were guests of a major international skin care manufacturer, called Shiseido Company. The company's CEO himself paid for our beautiful accommodations. He and three of his top executives took us out for a lovely dinner. One of them remarked at the similarities he saw between Armenian and Japanese songs. I began to share the story about my mother's miraculous deliverance as a child during that awful death march and described some of the ensuing miracles that occurred during the course of her life and mine.

My listeners were evidently amazed at what they were hearing and kept begging me to tell them more. I didn't want to dominate the conversation during our time together at that meal, but they kept opening the door and I kept going through. They were Shintoists, perhaps, or Buddhists, so I can't imagine what they thought about my stories of how Jesus Christ appeared so often in my life and performed such amazing miracles. I never had the slightest interest in preaching to them or telling them they had to receive Jesus as their personal savior. However, I pray God that they took something of my faith along with their memories of my stories.

A Life of Miracles

Prayer Healed Zabel's Cancer

While in Berkeley I met a fellow Armenian named Zabel. Her wealthy husband had recently divorced her, so Zabel moved to the Berkeley area to be near her parents. I knew she would be lonely, so I invited her to join our group. We would pray for each other and for others. Zabel didn't show up on a couple occasions, and I wondered why she hadn't called. One night her mother came to me in a dream and told me that Zabel had cancer. I dismissed the dream as a figment of my imagination, but the next day Zabel shared with us that she had throat cancer. She began crying and said they wanted to perform surgery. "Pray for me and for all of us," she said. The doctors said that the cancer had spread.

We had lunch together just before she was scheduled to be admitted to the hospital. I said to Zabel, "Can I pray for you?" I felt strongly moved that the Holy Spirit was telling me to pray for her at that time. We went outside the restaurant to be alone. I felt moved by my friend's pitiful situation—divorced, diseased, and frightened—and prayed fervently that the Lord would heal Zabel.

The next morning my phone rang around 7:00. It was the hospital. Zabel's ex-husband was on the other end of the line. He said that Zabel told him to call me with the news that the tumor had miraculously shrunk and the doctor's concluded the operation wasn't necessary, after all.

A Life of Miracles

Prayer Brought True Love "in Three Months" to My Son's Teacher

After moving to Berkeley, we bought a house in nearby El Cerrito and were enjoying life. We had come to love California and met some nice people. God laid a desire on my heart to find people who, like John, had left their first love for God and encourage them, like straying sheep, to return to His fold. When our younger son, Ronald, started first grade, I prayed, "I have time now, bring me people who loved you and left your presence, so I can call them back to you. Bring them to me. Let me share with them my husband's testimony."

My son's first grade teacher was the first person God brought to me in answer to my prayer. When we first met, I saw black clouds hanging over her spirit and a sadness in her heart that moved me to compassion. She seemed to me like a person who was thinking about ending her life.

"I see a lot of sadness in you," I said to her. "Is there something I can do for you?"

"How did you know that?"

"I can see it in your eyes and in your face. I would love to do something to help you. How can I help?"

She was amazed that I had picked up on her feelings.

I asked her to come have coffee with me the next day and she said she would love to accept the invitation. The next day I served us coffee and then asked, "What happened to you? Would you like to share with me?"

"I had been living with a man for eight years," she said. "He was going to marry me, but then he walked out. I am 37 years old. He took eight years of my life, and took my plans and dreams with him."

"Are you a Christian?" I asked.

"I had faith when I was young," she answered. "In fact, I was going to be a nun, but then I went away from the Lord and began checking out Eastern religions." Her reply moved my heart. I knew that God was answering my prayer. We spoke for a little while longer and I could tell that, like John had been, the woman was perfectly sincere in the midst of her doubts.

"With God all things are possible," I told her. "You loved Him before you can love Him again."

I frankly confessed to her that I was not a minister, but asked her if I could pray for her. "I am going to pray that God will give you the desire of His heart," I told the woman.

A Life of Miracles

We knelt together and as I prayed, I suddenly said, "O God bring someone to her in three months." I was as surprised as she must have been about the "three months." I had no idea where that came from. After we finished praying, I gave her a Bible and encouraged her to begin reading it. As she left, she thanked me for the tea and the prayer. She confessed that she was feeling better.

I didn't see the woman again for a while; but she was constantly on my mind and in my prayers. Then one day I stopped at the curb to pick Ronald up from school, and the teacher came running to my car. "Where have you been?" she asked. "Remember how I said that I was 37 and had nobody and you prayed that I would meet someone in three months? Well, my friend took me to a party. I was reluctant to go, but gave in. When we got there I got into conversation with a handsome man, who ended up asking me if we could go somewhere and have a coffee together. He is a Christian. We subsequently met a few other times, and two days ago he asked me to marry him."

She got married three months after the two of us had coffee and I made that strange prayer. The whole school rejoiced with her but none of them could have been as happy as I was because they didn't know the back-story about the promise we received from God. However, like the Woman At The Well in the famous Bible story, the woman couldn't keep the story to herself. She told the story to the director of the school and the rest of the teachers began to hear about what God had done.

After she was married, the woman wanted to have children. I invited her to come to my house where I told her, "Everything is possible. God can give you children. We will pray for children." I do not know why I said that; God led me.

The next time I saw her, she said. "Guess what! I am pregnant." The director was there at that meeting; we began rejoicing together.

A Life of Miracles

Prayer Prayer Led to a Perfect Home for "Ursula"

While in Berkeley we became close friends with Warren & Diane Willis. Warren was director of Campus Crusade for the California region. The couple would often come by our house for fellowship. Warren & Diane were transferred to Guam and a young couple came to take over the ministry. We'll pretend their names are Ed & Ursula. (I would tell you the man's real name, if I felt comfortable doing so, but I'm afraid of getting details wrong. Suffice to say, you would recognize the name, if I told you.)

Warren told John and me to take care of the new couple, so when Ed and his wife, Ursula, arrived, we welcomed them by hosting a rally at our house. The young people brought their musical instruments and sat on the floor singing and talking with each other while I fed everybody spaghetti. Ed and Ursula joined in the singing and the conversation.

After the young people left and Ed and Ursula were preparing to depart, I told them that I would help them with anything they needed. Ursula walked out to the car but suddenly told her husband to wait, came back to me, and said, "The Lord told me to come back and pray with you." It turned out that they were living in a small rental unit located in a shabby neighborhood. She said she had caught a peeping tom looking at her through the bathroom window and felt that they were in an unsafe situation. They really needed to find a more suitable place to live.

We talked about what she needed, and Ursula described in detail her ideal dwelling including such things as the number of bedrooms and the amount of money they could afford to pay. We knelt down and prayed together that God would give them the desires of their heart. We prayed fervently, specifically, and with hearts filled with hope.

That was on a Tuesday. On Sunday Ed & Ursula were with me in church when a fellow worshipper suddenly announced, "I'm selling my house. Who wants to buy it?" Of course, we asked for the details and it turned out that the house precisely matched the home of Ursula's dreams and our prayers. Furthermore, the asking price was the exact amount we had prayed for. Shortly afterwards, they were moving furniture and belongings into their new home.

A Life of Miracles

Prayer Led to a Life-changing Message in Guam

Not long after Warren & Diane moved to Guam, John and I were on our way to Japan for a conference, so we stopped in Guam to visit them. Two miracles occurred during our brief visit. The first occurred immediately after the plane landed at Guam International Airport. Diane was so glad to greet me at the airport! She gave me a big hug and then said. "I'm going to take you to meet some people. You are going to tell them your story. I told them all about you and they are thrilled to be able to meet you and to hear you speak."

I had just spent 12 hours on an international flight, so I weakly protested, "I'm tired, Diane!" I said. However, it was no use because 70 people were patiently waiting to hear the story of my life. As I got up to speak, I felt heavenly energy surging though my body and mind and began sharing with them the miracles that had occurred during my Cyprus upbringing and how God had brought me together with my husband in such a miraculous fashion. I explained to them how as a young girl I had determined never to marry anyone except the person that God would indicate was the man He had prepared for me.

The listeners were apparently moved by my account of the grace of God in my life because when I finished they rose to their feet and gave me a standing ovation. Afterwards, while I was speaking informally with a few who stayed behind to talk, one of them said that she was making an important decision about the man she was going to marry. She said that my story encouraged her to leave it in God's hand. I was thrilled because her comment indicated that God had been moving in her heart through my message. I was grateful that God had by His strength, empowered me to work through my weariness and to accomplish things for the sake of His kingdom.

A LIFE OF MIRACLES

Prayer Prayer Led to a Just-in-Time Miracle

A second miraculous event occurred while I was at Diane's house. We were speaking together about their struggles with the cost of living, etcetera. It turned out that they were on the point of running out of funds. Diane confided in me that her husband received no paycheck from Campus Crusade and they were forced to raise their own money for the ministry, which headquarters regarded as proof that they were serving where God wanted them.

She confessed to me how far in debt they were at the time and said that the demand for self-support often left them on the point of destitution. However, when they would come to the end of available funds, the exact amount they needed would suddenly show up.

I saw an example of the just-in-time deliverance that Diane was speaking about because while I was sitting with her at church that Sunday, a man came by and handed her an envelope that contained the exact sum of money that she told me she needed for their current bills.

Ani Amoore

I have provided help for people and have had them respond by saying some version of, "I really needed that today." I've given money on the spur of the moment to people who weren't asking for money and had them respond by telling me that it was exactly the amount they needed.

Prayers Brought My Family to America

One problem with America was that it was a long way from family and friends. We were the only Armenians in the area. On occasion, we would attend services at the First Presbyterian in Berkeley but were regular worshippers at St. Vartans Armenian Church in Oakland.

I especially missed my sister and told John that if we ever moved there, God would have to bring her to me, if He wanted us to be together. And that's just what happened.

God opened doors in miraculous ways so that a number of family members were able to join us and to experience The American Dream. My niece, Nevrig, was the first one to come. She was 20 years old and initially came from her Cyprus home on a study visa. The two of us prayed and agreed together that the Lord might open the door for her to secure permanent residency. I imagined that if she were able to immigrate, the rest of the family might be able to follow.

Ani Amoore

God doesn't always answer our prayers the way we expect. Nevrig got a job at Cowles Hospital, Berkeley, but met a fellow student—an Irishman. They were married, moved to Ireland, and have three wonderful children. However, even though Nevrig was living in the Emerald Isles instead of California, the other members of her family started to come. Her two brothers were first and then their mother, Varsen (my older sister), and her husband Kaspar. Varsen had taken such good care of our mother during Mom's sunset years that I was proud and gratified to be able to take care of her. One of Varsen's sons, Vartan, an acolyte in a London Church, came a few years later.

I don't have space to go into the details but, just as with Nevrig, each of them came because of doors that opened in seemingly miraculous response to specific prayers. Over the subsequent years, we noted the obvious hand of God at work. As each emigrant arrived, we thanked God—often with tears of gratitude in our eyes—for the miracle of their arrival. The micro migration of family members during those days was especially poignant because my father had never been able to return to the country he loved so much, but now his offspring were coming. Dad would have been so pleased!

A Life of Miracles

The miracles didn't stop following their arrival because the Lord who had brought them over took care of them once they got here. They kept settling down, getting good jobs, and buying houses in a sequence of events that involved one miracle after another. The Lord blessed the family, empowering us to become loving and happy in alignment with the legacy that we had received both from our Armenian culture and our Christian faith. We loved each other; we enjoyed times when we would get together.

The arrival of my sister, Varsen, was particularly happy for us. She and Kaspar moved in with John and me, and became part of our household. She was a real asset to the family—using her gifts as cook and housekeeper to keep us in good meals and to help keep our home clean and bright. We had four bedrooms in our home, so we managed easily. Five years later, they bought a lovely house of their own only ten minutes away.

Prayer Brought a Cousin Back from a Dark Valley

One day I got an anxious phone call from Garbis, my cousin who lived in England. He was very concerned because his son Armando, who was enrolled in college in Pennsylvania, had fallen out of contact. Garbis hadn't had mail from Armando in a long time and wasn't responding to Garbis' frantic phone calls. Finally, Garbis called begging me to pray for Armando and asking me to let him know as soon as I heard anything.

I went to my knees in prayer and asked God to move Armando to call me. The very next day, the phone rang, and I was delighted to hear Armando's voice on the other end of the line. "I'm sitting in front of a pancake house," Armando said. "Can you pick me up?" I was happy that God had answered my prayer in such a speedy manner.

We not only picked him up, but John and I let him stay with us while he unburdened himself. We learned that Armando had been in a deep depression because of an unfortunate affair with a woman. He felt that he had lost his true love and that life was no longer worth living. He was finally reaching out to me in an effort to make his way up and out of the dark valley that he had fallen into.

We both told him how much we loved him and how glad we were to help in his recovery. We shared with him our faith in Jesus Christ, as the one who can "heal the broken-hearted." After a couple weeks of spiritual recuperation, we took him to the airport and put him on a plane back to his school. Armando's recovery was complete and he remains to this day in fine spiritual and mental health. We were happy at how God had answered our prayer.

Ani Amoore

Prayer Brought a Husband into a Middle-Age Woman's Life

I met an Armenian woman 42 years ago at a dinner. After the meal, she pulled me aside and began telling me how miserable she was. She was a believer but was in her late 30s and wanted to have a child before she was 40. She didn't even have a boyfriend at that point. I had a sense that I should pray for her. I prayed that God would send the right man and that she would be able to have a child.

A few months later, the woman got a job, and met a tall, handsome Armenian. They fell in love and were married. We had a wedding shower. She called me up in front of the women and announced that I had prayed for her to be married, and God answered the prayer. She gave me time to speak. I praised the Lord and announced how God listens to our prayers when we are sincere. A year afterwards she gave birth to a beautiful child, and continued to tell everyone that God had answered prayer.

A LIFE OF MIRACLES

Prayer Did the Same Thing For a Daughter as for Her Mom

There is a curious ending to the story. The daughter grew into a lovely young woman, graduated from Harvard, and got a job in England in her profession. One day, while she was on a visit to America, the two of us were walking together. By that time the daughter was in her late 30s and said she wanted to be married and have a child before she was 40. It was like *déjà vu*; we were having the same conversation that her mom and I had so many years ago. I prayed with her, as I had prayed with her mom. God answered prayer and a year ago she married a handsome Armenian. We're waiting hopefully for a pregnancy to be announced soon.

Ani Amoore

Prayer Brought a Son to His Mother from Across an Ocean

During the Vietnam War, my sister, Varsen, left her son, Nazaret, behind in Cyprus in order to avoid the danger of being drafted into the Army. It was not a good situation. Varsen grieved over the separation, so I prayed fervently to God and subsequently had a strong conviction that Nazaret would not be drafted. I told my sister not to be afraid to bring him to America.

My advice was obviously risky because what if he came, was drafted after all, and then died on some battlefield? However, I didn't entertain the slightest misgiving because I had faith that I was under no illusion and that God really was speaking to me.

A LIFE OF MIRACLES

Prayer in Las Vegas Changed the Direction of a Life

Many memorable events in my life were simply the result of miraculous timing. I was in Las Vegas with my friend. We were looking at a menu outside Caesar's Palace when a young woman approached us and said, "It seems you have difficulty viewing the menu." She held up a small light to illuminate the menu for us. It was such a kind and unexpected gesture that an impulse came from someplace to invite her to join us at the meal. I told her that it would be my treat. She readily agreed.

As we chatted around the table, the young woman told us that she was traveling with her boyfriend. I shared with her my story about the suitors who had come around when I was young, and with my experience of waiting on the Lord to show me His will in a marriage partner before going forward with marriage—and that the Lord had then brought the perfect life partner to me. The young woman was touched by my story. "I'm going to think about what you said," she said. "I'm going to pray for God to show me His will before I consider marrying anyone."

I told her, "That's why we had dinner together. God brought us together so you could understand how to find His will."

A Life of Miracles

Prayer Put a Marriage Back Together Following Adultery

On more than one occasion, God has used me to reach out in healing fractured relationships. I am a close friend with a woman from Columbia who married the CEO of a major international corporation. The man was an immigrant from Russia. The woman and I would meet on a number of occasions and, as I found opportunity to do so, I would share my faith with her.

The woman was in an enviable position; she had everything her heart could wish for—homes, credit cards with no maximum, servants…. However, she came to me one day weeping bitter tears. "I walked into my home and found my husband in our bed with another woman." She was crying so hard that she could scarcely speak. She cut off relations with her husband and said that he could never see her again.

Her husband came to me. In a spirit of shame and remorse, he asked me to pray for him. He said that he still dearly loved his wife and would do anything to get her back. I told him that he had done a terrible thing.

He admitted that it was horrible and said that he would never do it again.

The possibility of reconciliation seemed unlikely in light of the man's deplorable behavior. However, I felt moved by the Spirit of God to call his wife. When she answered the phone, I told her what her husband had said. "He's going crazy with grief," I told her. "He wants to talk to you."

She agreed to meet him as long as the encounter would be conducted in a neutral place, which turned out to be my home. It would be difficult to imagine a better place than to attempt to find healing for wounded relationships. I had dedicated my home to the service of God and invoked His presence to dwell in every part of the structure. A spirit of tranquility hung about the place.

The couple met at the appointed time. After a brief period of greeting and opening conversation, they approached the difficult topic. The man met the wife's resentment and grief with a genuinely contrite heart and an attitude of sincere repentance. He fervently promised, "I will never do this again." Then he got down on his knees and took his wife's hands in his. "I love you very much," he said, "and promise you by Jesus and the Virgin Mary" that I will never do anything like this again."

A Life of Miracles

By the grace of God the couple succeeded in coming to a miraculous restitution. They are still happily married and living together in a home in Europe. They invited me on a number of occasions to visit them. It would have been nice to see their home, which I'm sure is spectacular, but I was busy at the time. It was enough simply to know that they were happily married. All praise to God that I could be His servant in providing for this miracle of reconciliation!

Ani Amoore

Prayer Sent Me an Angel, Bonnie Davey

Some people come into your life like angels sent from God. Bonnie Davey is one such person. Not long ago, my life was getting difficult, and I felt in need of someone to provide personal assistance. Nobody appropriate was available until one day when I was sitting in my wheelchair trying to think how to get to my car. I began praying for someone to come alongside to give me the help I needed. Suddenly a nice-looking woman was standing by my side. "Can I help you?" she asked. Then added, "You shouldn't be here in the sun. Let me help you to your car."

The woman seemed so pleasant and genuine that I wondered if she was the person God sent in answer to my prayer. Two weeks later, I called her. She was a caregiver and said that the man she had been caring for had passed away so she was suddenly free to help me. The answer to my prayer had dropped in my lap. "I need you!" I said. "I want you."

Bonnie comes in the morning and does what she can to help me face the day. She is generous and gracious. She seems to take joy and satisfaction from helping me. She has brought joy into my life. She listens attentively when I talk about my needs and feelings. She does grocery shopping for me. When I am in pain and depressed, Bonnie is there to lift me up.

The Lord brought me exactly who I needed at the precise moment when my need was greatest. My sense of being safely in God's hand is greater because Bonnie Davey keeps me in her thoughts and in her prayers.

Conclusion
Still Awash in Grace

The wonderful days of international adventures and service are ended, and I've retired to my pretty little home in Northern California where I am surrounded by flowers, trees, and sunshine. I am in my twilight years, but the fact is I am not yet finished worshipping God and serving the people around me.

I was still a vessel fit for the service of the King; a handmaiden of the Lord that He could still use for His glory and for the sake of His Kingdom! I hope and pray that people who read my book will not simply be entertained by my stories of how God has always been so real to me and has intervened in my life on so many occasions. I want to encourage people who read my book to reach out and to grab hold of faith for themselves. I'm trying to lead them to the point at which they can realize that no matter how powerful the darkness and evil pressing down on us, the power of God in the face of Jesus is greater still.

I pray especially that my children and other dear people in my life will read and will realize that God is near to each of them and that He answers prayer. If God could use me, He can use anybody who sincerely desires His will be done.

Perhaps years from now, when no memory is left of me on this earth except this book, my children's children through many generations will read and learn about how real the presence of God was to me and how wonderful it was to spend my lifetime in following His will and serving the people around me.

After all those years, perhaps my story will still encourage my distant descendants to discover the will of God to be powerful and sweet for themselves as I found it to be in my own experience.

That would surely be the best thing of all.

My life verse is, "In all your ways acknowledge him and he will direct your path."

He certainly has directed my path. Go to Him in faith, believe in Him without reservation, and He will direct your path too.

www.ingramcontent.com/pod-product-compliance
Lightning Source LLC
Chambersburg PA
CBHW071517080526
44588CB00011B/1462